T0119016

What are TOYS Made of?

by Joanna Brundle

©2016
Book Life
King's Lynn
Norfolk PE30 4LS

ISBN: 978-1-910512-87-6

All rights reserved
Printed in Spain

Written by:
Joanna Brundle

Designed by:
Drue Rintoul

A catalogue record for this book is available from the British Library.

CONTENTS

PAGE	Title
4	What is a Toy?
5	What is a Material?
6-7	Toys made of Plastic
8-9	Toys made of Wood
10-11	Toys made of Metal
12-13	Toys made of Glass and China
14-15	Toys made of Paper and Cardboard
16-17	Toys made of Cloth and Felt
18-19	Toys made of Other Things
20-21	Toys made of Recycled Materials
22-23	Fun Facts
24	Glossary and Index

You can find the **red** words in this book in the Glossary on page 24.

What is a TOY?

A toy is something which is made to be played with. Many different materials can be used to make toys.

All children enjoy playing with toys.

What is a MATERIAL?

A material is what something is made of. Many toys are made using plastic, wood or metal.

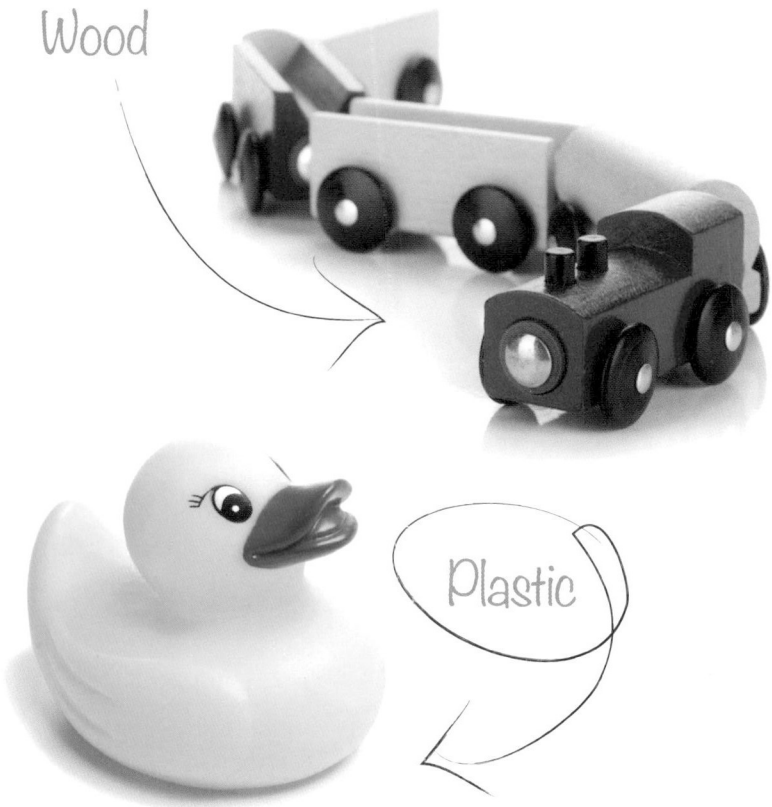

Toys made of
PLASTIC
Plastic is used to make toys because it is strong and light. It can be made into different shapes.
Building Bricks
Hula Hoop
Why do you think plastic is a good material for bath toys?

Many garden toys are made of plastic. This is because it is **waterproof** and it does not rot.
Swing & Slide
Sand Pit

Toys made of WOOD

Dolls House

Wood is a natural material. Toys made of wood last a long time because wood is strong and does not break easily.

Rocking Horse

Old-fashioned toys, like spinning tops and toy soldiers, were made of wood.

Toys made of METAL

Metal is used to make toys that need to be strong, like bicycles, scooters and pogo sticks.

Models of cars, fire engines and trains can be made using metal.

Toys made of GLASS AND CHINA

Marbles are made of coloured layers of glass. Some children collect marbles because they are very pretty.

Dolls used to be made of china. China breaks easily, so the children who played with them had to be gentle.

Toys made of PAPER AND CARDBOARD

Paper and cardboard are not as strong as plastic, wood or metal. Paper can be folded in special ways to make models.

Board games, like Ludo, are made of thick cardboard. Card games, like Snap, are made of thin card.

Children match the pictures on the board and the cards.

Toys made of CLOTH AND FELT

Soft toys are made from different kinds of cloth, like cotton and velour.

The bear is furry and soft. What other words could you use to describe the bear?

Puppets
Felt and cloth can be used to make puppets.
Here are some birds and cars made of felt. What else could you make?

Toys made of OTHER THINGS

Rubber is a natural material which is light and springy. It is great for making balls and bouncy toys.

In some countries, children make their toys from things they find. Pebbles can be used for throwing and catching.

Toys made of RECYCLED MATERIALS

Materials that can be **recycled**, like cardboard boxes, are great for making toys.

A dragon and car made from cardboard boxes.

An old tyre makes a fun garden swing.

You can paint plastic drinks bottles to make skittles.

Can you think of a toy to make by recycling?

FUN FACTS

1 The yo-yo is one of the oldest toys in the world. Yo-yo tricks include "Atom Smasher" and "Walk the Dog".

2 The first toy advertised on television was Mr Potato Head.

3 The ingredients of Play Doh are kept a secret.

4 The first teddy bears were made of real fur, with eyes of glass or leather.

GLOSSARY

BOARD GAME
A game played by moving pieces round a board

FELT
A fabric made of wool fibres pressed together

NATURAL
Something made by nature not humans

OLD-FASHIONED
Not modern

RECYCLED
Something old that has been reused to make something new

RUBBER
A natural, stretchy material, made of tree sap or juice

VELOUR
A fabric with a very soft feel

WATERPROOF
Something that water cannot pass through

INDEX

CARDBOARD 14, 15, 20
MATERIAL 4, 5, 8, 18
METAL 5, 10, 11, 14
MODELS 11, 14
PLASTIC 5, 6, 7, 11, 14, 21
STRONG 6, 10, 14
WOOD 5, 8, 9, 14

Photocredits: Abbreviations: l-left, r-right, b-bottom, t-top, c-centre, m-middle.
All images are courtesy of Shutterstock.com.

Front Cover – kai keisuke. 1 – AkeSak. 2 – ConstantinosZ. 3bl – Hayati Kayhan. 3br – Gyvafoto. 3r – NeoBuu. 3tr – Lasse Kristensen. 4bl – Max Topchii. 4tr – Jacek Chabraszewski. 5tr – Szasz-Fabian Ilka Erika. 5c, 20br – Evgeny Karandaev. 5bl – r.classen. 6bl – Nenov Brothers Images. 6 – Carlos Horta. 7 – CroMary. 7instet – Vichy Deal. 8 – Olivier Le Queinec. 8inset – Ingrid Balabanova. 9r – Nicole Gordine. 9bl – kai keisuke. 10l – Ljupco Smokovski. 10r – Sergei Kolesnikov. 11 – Twin Design. 12 – STILLFX. 12inset – auremar. 13r – Sedin. 13bl – Belinda Pretorius. 14 – Vladimir Melnikov. 15 – Dmitri-Maruta. 16 – grekoff. 17 – Zdenek Rosenthaler. 17bl – sattva78. 18l – Johan Swanepoel. 18br – Todd Taulman. 19 – Pavel L Photo and Video. 19tl – Volt Collection. 20 – Kiselev Andrey Valerevich. 21 – Blend Images 21bl – Africa Studio. 22 tr – Winston Link. 22bl – PAISAN HOMHUAN. 23 – Robyn Mackenzie. 23tl – George Burba.